inspire
for teachers

Prayers, Promises, and Proverbs
for Those Who Change Lives and Touch Hearts

by
Dr. Josie Washington Carr, Ed.D.

The Lord God hath given me the tongue of the learned,
that I should know how to speak a word in season...he
wakeneth mine ear to hear as the learned.

Isaiah 50:4

Harrison House
Tulsa, Oklahoma

17 16   10 9 8 7

Inspire for Teachers: Prayers, Promises, and Proverbs
for Those Who Change Lives and Touch Hearts
ISBN 13: 978-1-57794-884-1
ISBN 10: 1-57794-884-X
Copyright © 2008 by Jostan Publications, Inc.
PO Box 672514
Houston, Texas 77267

Published by Harrison House, Inc.
PO Box 35035
Tulsa, Oklahoma 74153
www.harrisonhouse.com

Dedication

This book is dedicated to:

My loving mother, Mildred Irvin, who taught me to trust God, no matter what, and to pray everyday because *"prayer changes things."*

My parents-in-love, Jackie and Gladys Carr, who love me as their very own.

My husband, Dr. Stanley B. Carr, who continues to prove his love for me and his belief in me.

My children, Jarvis and Jakia Carr, who are like olive vines round about my table and the reasons for this book.

My sisters: Mary Truehill, Lilly Washington, Dianna Myles, and Cynthia Ellioe; and brothers: Kevin Washington, Calvin Washington, and Kenneth Norwood.

My pastors, Drs. I.V. and Bridget Hilliard, who teach me the uncompromising Word of God.

My friends and traveling buddies, Patrice Mayes, Beverly Newsome, and Ann Wilson.

My professors at Texas Southern University who refused to give up on me.

My teachers, family, and friends in Donaldsonville, Louisiana.

And to all educators with whom God has allowed me to work and supervise. You have proven, with a vision and a committed team, God can and will do the impossible in the lives of students.

Special Acknowledgements

Everything I have accomplished in this life has been done with the assistance of others. I want to express my sincere gratitude to several people without whose help this book would have remained only a thought.

Special thanks to my pastor, Dr. I.V. Hilliard, whose teaching has changed my life and to my first lady, Dr. Bridget Hilliard, who taught me how to pray and confess the Word of God over my situations. Thank you for believing in me. Because of the awesome impact you have made in my life, students, parents, and educators are being blessed all over the world.

I want to give a super-duper thanks to Pastor Sheldon Reed, who assisted me by willingly sharing his wisdom and recollection of Scriptures' content and meaning. Your encouragement has blessed my life.

A loving thanks to my staff—pastors Reginald Petitt, Derrell Foster, Thomas Foster, James Mitchell, Earline Pruitt, Brenda Mitchell, Laura Mitchell, Beverly Burkett, Denise Collie, Chester Jenkins, and Filecha Lucas—for your commitment to excellence, teamwork, and professionalism. You are a source of inspiration to me.

Thanks to Filecha Lucas, Hazel Hughes, and Ron Marshall for your assistance in bringing this project to completion.

Table of Contents

Foreword

You are about to embark upon a true blessing. Josie and I are professional educators and have been married for twenty years. I am not sure if I drove her to praying or if she just found out somehow that she should always pray.

For twenty years, Josie has been committed to praying the Word of God concerning our situations. Her prayer results are very impressive. She has experienced the supernatural healing of students and a staff member healed from multiple sclerosis and minor paralysis. She has been healed from sickness and disease, physically and emotionally. We have two children the doctors said we would not have. Josie climbed the success ladder in education, ranging from teacher to executive director, in a reasonable time frame. Against all odds, she completed her doctoral degree. And lastly, we are still married.

This masterpiece, *Inspire for Teachers,* is relevant, exciting, and informative. I encourage you to use this book as a reference resource. Glean from the insights and pray the prayers for yourself and others you know in the field of education. I believe you will experience a renewal as you witness the Word of God changing situations, at school and at home, on your behalf.

—*Dr. Stanley B. Carr*

Foreword

Committed! Compelling! Creative! Just a few words to describe this educator and the quality of work she has produced in the classroom, as an administrator, and now as an author. *Inspire for Teachers* is a timely treasure that shares practical as well as biblical insights regarding the student, teacher, and school leader.

Dr. Carr highlights a clear pathway that leads to the answers to many of the challenges we face in education. The framework for this book was birthed from the author's own vivid experience of discovering the reality of the Word of God applied to your everyday encounters. It is obvious that she searched the Scriptures and discovered a treasure of instruction and encouragement to share with the world and those in her profession.

As her first principal and district superintendent, it is an honor to recommend this dynamic masterpiece, *Inspire for Teachers*, to the world and to every teacher, student, parent, and school leader.

—*Dr. Joseph A. Drayton, Ed.D.*
Past president of the National Alliance of
Black School Educators (NABSE)
Former district superintendent for
Houston Independent School District

Introduction

This book was written to assist teachers and educational leaders in all facets of education. Whether you are working in grade school, college, adult education, or vocational training, these prayers, insights, and confessions will help you to persevere to the completion of your desired goal.

I believe the foundation of knowledge is the Word of God. It is from the basis of this foundation that every issue concerning school is addressed, corrected, modified, enhanced, or eliminated.

The Word tells us to imitate God as dear children. According to Hebrews 11:3, "The worlds were framed by the word of God." He spoke His world into existence and if we are to imitate Him, we must do likewise. Romans 10:9-10 tells us to believe in our heart and confess with our mouth. It goes on to say, "Confession is made unto...." Mark 11:23 tells us that we will have what we say. As teachers and educational leaders, we must believe what the Word of God says about us and confess or speak that Word with our mouths. God *will* watch over His Word to perform it in our lives.

It is my desire for you to stand firm on the Word of God and overcome every hindering force that would attempt to derail your destiny.

I believe *prayer* is fundamental for success in every area of a Christian's life. As we look into the basic instruction book for living on earth (the Bible), we find it to be the cornerstone in the lives of Jesus and the apostles.

Paul spent many hours interceding for new believers. In Ephesians 1:16 he wrote, "[I] cease not to give thanks for you, making mention of you in my prayers." In Colossians 1:3 he said, "We give thanks to God and the Father of our Lord Jesus Christ, praying always for you." Luke 18:1 says men ought always to pray and not faint. Prayer is the key to overcoming life's situations. It is the fuel that ignites and maintains the passion to persevere and win.

According to 1 Corinthians 1:4-9, God does not want you, as an educator, to lack in any area of your life. "I thank my God always on your behalf, for the grace of God which is given you by Jesus Christ; that in everything ye are enriched by him, in all utterance, and in all knowledge; even as the testimony of Christ was confirmed in you: so that you come behind in no gift; waiting for the coming of our Lord Jesus Christ:

who shall also confirm you unto the end, that ye may be blameless in the day of our Lord Jesus Christ. God is faithful, by whom ye were called unto the fellowship of his Son Jesus Christ our Lord."

God always answers prayer in the affirmative when it is based on His Word. He told us to put Him in remembrance of His Word. 1 John 5:14-15 tells us when we pray or ask anything according to God's will, we can have confidence that He has heard us and we have the petitions that we desire of Him. Jeremiah 1:12 says God will hasten His Word to perform it. God's Word is the answer to your problem.

This book contains prayers and confessions based on the Word of God that will bring victory to your situation. Scriptures have been provided for reference and study purposes.

Successful Teachers

What would education be without a *teacher?* Someone once said, "A teacher impacts eternity; one never knows when his influence will end." Luke 6:40 states when a child is fully trained, he will be like his teacher.

Having been a teacher for several years, I have heard and read many sayings that relate to teaching: "Teachers have class"; "To teach is to touch a life forever"; "A teacher preserves the past, reveals the present, and creates the future." All of these are great, but the greatest saying concerning a teacher is found in the Bible, John 3:2, where it is referring to Jesus and says, "Thou art a teacher come from God."

This Scripture validates who you are as an educator. It brings encouragement on those days when you feel nothing is going right, no one else cares, and it is just not worth it! Remember Jesus had twelve students (disciples) and it did not go perfectly for Him. His students just did not get it sometimes. He taught in parables, gave them object lessons, practicums, and evaluations, but still in the Scriptures we see where Jesus always had to reteach a lesson because some did not get it the first time. *Does any of this sound familiar?*

Not only that, Jesus had students with special needs: Peter and Judas. I believe Peter, because of his behavior, would be in a behavior modification program. At times, he was very unstable and unpredictable. Judas was a thief and in our day, he would be in an alternative school or a juvenile detention center.

This Scripture (John 3:2) informs you of the simple fact that teaching is not just a profession; it is a *calling* from God. He wants to use you to impact the lives of the students He has placed in your care. If no one else cares, you do; and because you are called of God and depending on Him, you will make the difference in the lives of your students.

As I mentioned earlier, Jesus' students were not perfect, but He loved them and continued to teach and pray for them. Jesus expected the disciples to get and operate in the principles He taught. In John 8:31-32, He admonishes them to continue in what He has taught, which would cause them to know the truth; and the truth that they know would make them free.

God is counting on you to teach your students. Continue to encourage them to study and increase in knowledge, because that which they know can never be taken away, only built upon, and will cause them to be free from poverty, failure, dropping out, etc.

"You are a teacher, come from God." May the following prayers, Scriptures, and confessions assist you in your endeavors to please God with your life, and be the teacher He has called you to be.

Prayers for Teachers

A Teacher's Daily Prayer

Father, in the name of Jesus, I praise You for who You are and for who You have called me to be. Thank You for Your Word that declares I can come boldly to the throne of grace and obtain mercy to help me in my time of need. I believe that You are concerned about me and my profession. As an educator, I pray Your Word and You watch over it to perform it in my situation. I am grateful for the privilege to be an instrument in Your hand to impact the lives of students, parents, teachers, and school leaders.

I ask You to help me to do my job as unto You and not unto man. Help my teaching to be seasoned with Your love for all my students regardless of race, creed, or socio-economic background. Father, because You are working in and through me to do Your pleasure, my students will soar above their peers academically, socially, and behaviorally. Because You love them so greatly through me, they will come to know Jesus and receive Him as their Lord and Savior. I pray that I am a daily reflection of Your love, discipline, kindness, forgiveness, wisdom, strength, and success to all my students and others that You cause to cross my path.

As a colleague to other teachers, principals, and school leaders, I pray and believe according to 2 Timothy 2:24-26 (AMP), I am not quarrelsome but kind and mild-tempered with everyone. I am a skilled and suitable teacher, patient, forbearing, and willing to suffer wrong. I correct my colleagues with courtesy and gentleness, in hope that You would cause them to repent and come to know the truth. Father, You are not a respecter of persons, and what You have done for one, You will do for another. Therefore I thank You for helping me to support, applaud, and appreciate the accomplishments of others, knowing whatever good thing I do for others, You will cause it to happen for me, in Jesus' name, Amen.

Scriptures for Study

Let us therefore come boldly unto the throne of grace, that we may obtain mercy, and find grace to help in time of need.

Hebrews 4:16

Then said the Lord unto me, Thou hast well seen: for I will hasten my word to perform it.

Jeremiah 1:12

And whatsoever ye do, do it heartily, as to the Lord, and not unto men.

Colossians 3:23

And the servant of the Lord must not be quarrelsome (fighting and contending). Instead, he must be kindly to everyone and mild-tempered [preserving the bond of peace]; he must be a skilled and suitable teacher, patient and forbearing and willing to suffer wrong. He must correct his opponents with courtesy and gentleness, in the hope that God may grant that they will repent and come to know the Truth [that they will perceive and recognize and become accurately acquainted with and acknowledge it], and that they may come to their senses [and] escape out of the snare of the devil, having been held captive by him, [henceforth] to do His [God's] will.

2 Timothy 2:24-26 (AMP)

Knowing that whatsoever good thing any man doeth, the same shall he receive of the Lord, whether he be bond or free.

Ephesians 6:8

Confidence

Father, in the name of Jesus, I come before You in faith, praising and thanking You for Your faithfulness to confirm Your Word with signs following.

I believe and confess I approach each day and assignment with confidence, knowing that You have begun a good work in me and will perform it until the day of Jesus Christ. I boldly declare You as my helper and I choose not to fear or be terrified of anything. I know that success is not merely achieved by my might nor by my power but by Your Spirit working in and through me.

Father, thank You that there is nothing too hard for You. Even when it seems there is no way out of my situation, I rejoice knowing You always cause me to triumph in Christ Jesus. I confidently say, You are my strength and You will make my feet like hinds' feet and cause me to walk upon high places, in Jesus' name, Amen.

Scriptures for Study

And they went forth, and preached every where, the Lord working with them, and confirming the word with signs following. Amen.

Mark 16:20

Being confident of this very thing, that he which hath begun a good work in you will perform it until the day of Jesus Christ.

Philippians 1:6

Then he answered and spake unto me, saying, This is the word of the Lord unto Zerubbabel, saying, Not by might, nor by power, but by my spirit, saith the Lord of hosts.

Zechariah 4:6

Now thanks be unto God, which always causeth us to triumph in Christ, and maketh manifest the savour of his knowledge by us in every place.

2 Corinthians 2:14

Ah Lord God! behold, thou hast made the heaven and the earth by thy great power and stretched out arm, and there is nothing too hard for thee.

Jeremiah 32:17

The Lord God is my strength, and he will make my feet like hinds' feet, and he will make me to walk upon mine high places.

Habakkuk 3:19

Finances

Father, thank You for Your Word that will not return void but accomplishes what it says and prospers in the situation in which I send it.

I confess Your Word with my mouth and believe in my heart that because I honor You with my tithe and offering, I experience the windows of heaven's blessings (favor, insight, and financial increase) in my life. I believe every need is met with heaven's best and that You have given me everything that pertains to life and godliness.

I will not take a (worrying) thought, but will continue to seek first the kingdom of God, and those things will be added to me. I declare, I will not lack any beneficial thing, in Jesus' name, Amen.

Scriptures for Study

So shall my word be that goeth forth out of my mouth: it shall not return unto me void, but it shall accomplish that which I please, and it shall prosper in the thing whereto I sent it.

Isaiah 55:11

Bring ye all the tithes into the storehouse, that there may be meat in mine house, and prove me now herewith, saith the Lord of hosts, if I will not open you the windows of heaven, and pour you out a blessing, that there shall not be room enough to receive it.

Malachi 3:10

But my God shall supply all your need according to his riches in glory by Christ Jesus.

Philippians 4:19

According as his divine power hath given unto us all things that pertain unto life and godliness, through the knowledge of him that hath called us to glory and virtue.

2 Peter 1:3

Therefore take no thought, saying, What shall we eat? or, What shall we drink? or, Wherewithal shall we be clothed? (For after all these things do the Gentiles seek:) for your heavenly Father knoweth that ye have need of all these things. But seek ye first the kingdom of God, and his righteousness; and all these things shall be added unto you.

Matthew 6:31-33

Recovery From Mistakes

Father, I acknowledge and confess that I sinned against You and _____ when I did _____. Thank You for Your Word that declares I can confess my sin and You are faithful to forgive me and cleanse me from all unrighteousness. Thank You for forgiving and cleansing me; therefore, I am in right standing with You.

I now plead the blood of Jesus over my mind regarding this matter. I renounce any harm, ill-feeling, or disadvantage this may have caused to others. Thank You for the comforting ministry of the Holy Spirit on their behalf.

It is my desire to please You with my life; there-fore, I ask You to create in me a clean heart and renew a right spirit within me. Restore unto me the joy of Your salvation and uphold me with Your free spirit.

Scriptures for Study

If we confess our sins, he is faithful and just to forgive us our sins, and to cleanse us from all unrighteousness.

1 John 1:9

Create in me a clean heart, O God; and renew a right spirit within me. Restore unto me the joy of thy salvation; and uphold me with thy free spirit. Then will I teach transgressors thy ways; and sinners shall be converted unto thee.

Psalm 51:10,12-13

Promotion

Father, in Jesus' name, Your Word says promotions do not come from the east, nor the west, nor the south, but God is the judge who puts down one and picks up another.

I believe You perfect everything that concerns me; therefore, according to Your Word, You are elevating me to a higher level of living. Thank You for causing my name, application, and resume to rise to the top so that those in authority to make decisions will call me. Because Your Word says the king's heart is in Your hand, I believe and confess _____'s heart is in Your hand and You are turning it towards me concerning this situation. I believe and confess this promotion will cause me to prosper and I will have more to give to the kingdom of God.

Thank You for raising up someone, somewhere, to use his/her power, ability, and influence to help me, and for the creativity and wisdom necessary to fulfill my new assignment.

I live in daily expectation of doors of opportunity opening for me, in Jesus' name, Amen!

Scriptures for Study

For promotion cometh neither from the east, nor from the west, nor from the south. But God is the judge: he putteth down one, and setteth up another.

Psalm 75:6-7

The Lord will perfect that which concerneth me: thy mercy, O Lord, endureth for ever: forsake not the works of thine own hands.

Psalm 138:8

The king's heart is in the hand of the Lord, as the rivers of water: he turneth it whithersoever he will.

Proverbs 21:1

If any of you lack wisdom, let him ask of God, that giveth to all men liberally, and upbraideth not; and it shall be given him.

James 1:5

Protection

Father, in Jesus' name, thank You for watching over Your Word to perform it in my life. Thank You for permitting me to dwell in the secret place of the Most High and abide under the shadow of the Almighty.

You are my refuge and my fortress. When I need shelter, You are my mighty high tower and my place of safety. I am safe in You. You are my God and in You and You alone do I put my trust. Surely, You shall deliver me from the snare of the fowler and from the noisome pestilence. Your Word is my shield and buckler.

Father, thank You that You have not given me a spirit of fear; therefore, I am not afraid of the terror by night, nor of the arrow that flies by day, nor of the pestilence that walks in darkness, nor of the destruction that wastes at noonday. A thousand may fall at my side and ten thousand at my right hand but it shall not come nigh me. Only with my eyes will I behold and see the reward of the wicked.

Because I have made You my habitation, there shall no evil befall me; neither shall any plague come near my dwelling. Thank You, Father, for giving

Your angels charge over me to keep me in all my ways. They shall bear me up in their hands so that I do not dash my foot against a stone. I tread upon the enemy. He is under my feet.

Father, I set my love upon You; therefore, You deliver me and set me on high because I know Your name. When I call upon You, You will answer me and be with me in trouble. You will deliver me and honor me. With long life, You will satisfy me and show me Your salvation.

Father, You are my confidence and You keep my foot from being caught in a trap or hidden danger. Thank You, Father, that no weapon that is formed against me will prosper and every tongue that rises against me shall be condemned. Thank You, Father, for redeeming my life from destruction, and protecting me from accidents, in Jesus' name, Amen.

Scriptures for Study

He that dwelleth in the secret place of the most High shall abide under the shadow of the Almighty. I will say of the Lord, He is my refuge and my fortress: my God; in him will I trust. Surely he shall deliver thee from the snare of the fowler, and from the noisome pestilence. He shall cover thee with his feathers, and under his wings shalt thou trust: his truth shall be thy shield and buckler. Thou shalt not be afraid for the terror by night; nor for the arrow that flieth by day; nor for the pestilence that walketh in darkness; nor for the destruction that wasteth at noonday. A thousand shall fall at thy side, and ten thousand at thy right hand; but it shall not come nigh thee. Only with thine eyes shalt thou behold and see the reward of the wicked. Because thou hast made the Lord, which is thy refuge, even the most High, thy habitation; there shall no evil befall thee, neither shall any plague come nigh thy dwelling. For he shall give his angels charge over thee, to keep thee in all thy ways. They shall bear thee up in their hands, lest thou dash thy foot against a stone. Thou shalt tread upon the lion and adder: the young lion and the dragon shalt thou trample under feet. Because he hath set his love upon me, therefore will I deliver him: I will set him on high, because he hath known my name. He shall call upon me, and I will answer him: I will be with him in trouble; I will deliver him, and honour

him. With long life will I satisfy him, and shew
him my salvation.

Psalm 91:1-16

Then said the Lord unto me, Thou hast well seen:
for I will hasten my word to perform it.

Jeremiah 1:12

No weapon that is formed against thee shall
prosper; and every tongue that shall rise against
thee in judgment thou shalt condemn. This is the
heritage of the servants of the Lord, and their
righteousness is of me, saith the Lord.

Isaiah 54:17

Who redeemeth thy life from destruction; who
crowneth thee with lovingkindness and tender
mercies.

Psalm 103:4

For the Lord shall be thy confidence, and shall
keep thy foot from being taken.

Proverbs 3:26

Unity

Father, thank You for the mind to work and the discipline to finish every task assigned to us. We have confidence that if we ask anything according to Your Word, You hear us and grant the petition(s) we desire of You.

Father, we believe we are of one mind and language; therefore, nothing will be withheld from us that we imagine to do. All our visions and dreams come to full maturity in Jesus' name.

Holy Spirit, You have freedom in our lives. Teach, lead, and guide us according to the perfect will of the Father. We are vessels of honor ready for the master's use.

Father, we commit to not only be of one mind, but to also have compassion for one another and love as sisters and brothers, treating each other with kindness and courtesy.

Thank You, Father, that there is no jealousy, envy, or strife among us and we esteem each other highly. We do not render evil for evil but, on the contrary, blessing, knowing that whatever good we do for someone else, we will receive the same from the Lord.

Father, we declare Your perfect will is done in us and through us, in Jesus' name, Amen.

Scriptures for Study

And this is the confidence that we have in him, that, if we ask any thing according to his will, he heareth us: and if we know that he hear us, whatsoever we ask, we know that we have the petitions that we desired of him.

1 John 5:14-15

And the Lord said, Behold, the people is one, and they have all one language; and this they begin to do: and now nothing will be restrained from them, which they have imagined to do.

Genesis 11:6

Finally, be ye all of one mind, having compassion one of another, love as brethren, be pitiful, be courteous: not rendering evil for evil, or railing for railing: but contrariwise blessing; knowing that ye are thereunto called, that ye should inherit a blessing.

1 Peter 3:8-9

Hath not the potter power over the clay, of the same lump to make one vessel unto honour, and another unto dishonour?

Romans 9:21

That they all may be one; as thou, Father, art in me, and I in thee, that they also may be one in us: that the world may believe that thou hast sent me. And the glory which thou gavest me I have given them; that they may be one, even as we are one.

John 17: 21-22

Knowing that whatsoever good thing any man doeth, the same shall he receive of the Lord, whether he be bond or free.

Ephesians 6:8

Prayers for
Your Students

Academic Excellence

This is the day that the Lord has made; I choose to rejoice and be glad in it. Father, I pause to give You thanks for who You are in my life and in the lives of all my students.

As my students and I start this day, I declare they are disciples taught of the Lord and obedient to Your will. Great is the peace of my students and undisturbed is their composure.

I pray and believe my students choose to obey Your Word and to submit to those in authority over them. They choose to respect their parents and teachers. They use wisdom and make the right choices in every situation. They speak only that which is good and beneficial. They please You with their thoughts, words, and actions as they walk in integrity of heart.

Thank You, Father, that my students have the mind to stay focused in all their academic endeavors. They are ten times wiser than the children of the world. They are the head and not the tail. They are above only and not beneath, blessed coming in and going out.

I pray and confess that my students find favor, good understanding, and high esteem with God, their parents, classmates, and other staff members. I believe, as I stand before them as a vessel being used of You, that they will cultivate an appreciation for education and living a life that is pleasing to God, in Jesus' name, Amen.

Scriptures for Study

This is the day which the Lord hath made; we will rejoice and be glad in it.

Psalm 118:24

And all thy children shall be taught of the Lord; and great shall be the peace of thy children.

Isaiah 54:13

Children, obey your parents in the Lord: for this is right. Honour thy father and mother; which is the first commandment with promise; that it may be well with thee, and thou mayest live long on the earth.

Ephesians 6:1-3

Let no corrupt communication proceed out of your mouth, but that which is good to the use of edifying, that it may minister grace unto the hearers.

Ephesians 4:29

And in all matters of wisdom and understanding, that the king enquired of them, he found them ten times better than all the magicians and astrologers that were in all his realm.

Daniel 1:20

And the Lord shall make thee the head, and not the tail; and thou shalt be above only, and thou shalt not be beneath; if that thou hearken unto the commandments of the Lord thy God, which I command thee this day, to observe and to do them.

Deuteronomy 28:13

And Jesus increased in wisdom and stature, and in favour with God and man.

Luke 2:52

Anger

Father, thank You because _____
(student's name) is Your child. He/she chooses to put aside all anger and strife. God, I speak peace to the raging thoughts that may flood his/her mind. Devil, I command you to take your hands off _____; he/she is set apart for the work of God. Anger, you will not destroy _____. He/she is the seed of the righteous and delivered from every trick of the devil.

Father, because You promised that You would never break Your covenant nor alter the thing that has gone out of Your lips, I pray and believe that _____ operates in the peace of God that surpasses all understanding and keeps his/her heart and mind quiet through Christ Jesus. I declare the peace of God and a calm spirit overshadow _____ in every situation, and cause him/her to act accordingly.

I confess, _____ is kind to everyone. He/she is tenderhearted, willing to forgive others just as God has forgiven him/her. He/she makes the quality decision to put aside all bitterness, wrath, anger, uproar, and evil speaking. I believe, therefore I speak, _____ (student's name) is swift to hear, slow to speak, and slow to wrath, so that the light of Jesus will shine upon his/her path.

Father, thank You for allowing me to be a part of _____'s life and to show him/her a better way to handle anger and frustration. Thank You for the wisdom to handle this situation in a firm but loving manner. _____ (student's name) is a student of great peace, purpose, and productivity, in Jesus' name, Amen.

Scriptures for Study

Let no corrupt communication proceed out of your mouth, but that which is good to the use of edifying, that it may minister grace unto the hearers. And grieve not the holy Spirit of God, whereby ye are sealed unto the day of redemption. Let all bitterness, and wrath, and anger, and clamour, and evil speaking, be put away from you, with all malice: and be ye kind one to another, tender-hearted, forgiving one another, even as God for Christ's sake hath forgiven you.

Ephesians 4:29-32

inspire for teachers

Wherefore, my beloved brethren, let every man be swift to hear, slow to speak, slow to wrath.

James 1:19

He that is slow to wrath is of great understanding: but he that is hasty of spirit exalteth folly.

Proverbs 14:29

A wrathful man stirreth up strife: but he that is slow to anger appeaseth strife.

Proverbs 15:18

He that is slow to anger is better than the mighty; and he that ruleth his spirit than he that taketh a city.

Proverbs 16:32

Nevertheless my lovingkindness will I not utterly take from him, nor suffer my faithfulness to fail. My covenant will I not break, nor alter the thing that is gone out of my lips.

Psalm 89:33-34

Fear

Dear God, what a privilege to come before Your throne of grace on behalf of my students. Father, You are love and You are perfect. Thank You that perfect love casts out all fear. Therefore, I pray and believe that You love my student,_____(student's name), through me; and because of that perfect love he/she chooses not to fear, nor allow his/her heart to be troubled or afraid. There is no fear in love; and You have not given him/her a spirit of fear, but of power, love, and a sound mind.

I speak to the forces of darkness in the mighty name of Jesus! I call your assignment of fear to naught against _____ (student's name) and I command you to take your hands off _____ (student's name) because he/she is God's property. I plead the blood of Jesus over _____ and declare no evil shall come nigh _____ or nigh his/her dwelling. God has given His angels charge over _____, and the angels will keep _____ safe in all his /her ways.

I believe my student, _____, will approach every assignment and endeavor with confidence, which will cause his/her grades, classroom participation, and conduct to excel.

Thank You, Father, I see my student, _____, functioning in the peace of God as he/she becomes the person of purpose and great productivity that You have called him/her to be, in Jesus' name, Amen.

Scriptures for Study

For God hath not given us the spirit of fear; but of power, and of love, and of a sound mind.

2 Timothy 1:7

There is no fear in love; but perfect love casteth out fear: because fear hath torment. He that feareth is not made perfect in love.

1 John 4:18

There shall no evil befall thee, neither shall any plague come nigh thy dwelling. For he shall give his angels charge over thee, to keep thee in all thy ways.

Psalm 91:10-11

Student Experiencing a Health Challenge

Father, in Jesus' name, I believe _____ (student's name) is healed by the stripes of Jesus. Jesus bore his/her sickness on the tree; therefore, with boldness I command sickness to flee _____'s body. Every symptom must cease and leave _____'s body now, in the name of Jesus.

Father, I thank You that Your Word is medicine to _____'s body and life to his/her flesh. I see him/her walking in divine health all the days of his/her life.

I send Your Word that says You heal all our diseases and _____ shall live and not die and declare the works of the Lord. I believe his/her health is springing forth speedily and _____ will continue to be a person of divine purpose and great productivity, in Jesus' name, Amen.

Scriptures for Study

Who his own self bare our sins in his own body on the tree, that we, being dead to sins, should live unto righteousness: by whose stripes ye were healed.

1 Peter 2:24

My son, attend to my words; incline thine ear unto my sayings. Let them not depart from thine eyes; keep them in the midst of thine heart. For they are life unto those that find them, and health to all their flesh. Keep thy heart with all diligence; for out of it are the issues of life.

Proverbs 4:20-23

Bless the Lord, O my soul, and forget not all his benefits: who forgiveth all thine iniquities; who healeth all thy diseases.

Psalm 103:2-3

Because thou hast made the Lord, which is my refuge, even the most High, thy habitation; there shall no evil befall thee, neither shall any plague come nigh thy dwelling.

Psalm 91:9-10

Rebellion

Father, in Jesus' name, I speak Your Word over _____ (student's name), who is temporarily experiencing a rebellious attitude. I pray, believe, and confess that he/she submits to God, resists the devil, and that the devil flees from him/her.

Father, Your Word declares that rebellion is as the sin of witchcraft and stubbornness is as iniquity and idolatry. Therefore, in the name of Jesus, I command the spirit of rebellion to cease and desist in its maneuver against _____. I pray and believe that he/she is protected by the blood of Jesus, delivered from the powers of darkness and walking in the divine peace of God. I believe he/she will choose to be obedient and eat the good of the land, and obey and be submissive to those who are in authority over him/her and watch for his/her soul.

The opening of my lips shall be to speak the Word of God over _____, declaring he/she is a student of excellence, great peace, and divine productivity, in Jesus' name, Amen.

Scriptures for Study

Submit yourselves therefore to God. Resist the devil, and he will flee from you.

James 4:7

If ye be willing and obedient, ye shall eat the good of the land.

Isaiah 1:19

Verily I say unto you, Whatsoever ye shall bind on earth shall be bound in heaven: and whatsoever ye shall loose on earth shall be loosed in heaven.

Matthew 18:18

Obey them that have the rule over you, and submit yourselves: for they watch for your souls, as they that must give account, that they may do it with joy, and not with grief: for that is unprofitable for you.

Hebrews 13:17

Who hath delivered us from the power of darkness, and hath translated us into the kingdom of his dear Son.

Colossians 1:13

Low Self-Esteem

Father, in Jesus' name, I thank You for _____ (student's name), and that he/she is a disciple taught of the Lord, obedient to God's will, with great peace and undisturbed composure.

Father, thank You that _____ can do all things through Christ who strengthens him/her. He/she has the mind of Christ and holds the thoughts, feelings, and purposes of God's heart. He/she does not fret or have anxiety about anything.

The Word of God dwells richly in _____, and He who has begun a good work in him/her will continue to perform it until the day of Jesus Christ. The joy of the Lord is his/her strength, and he/she is experiencing the peace of God in every situation of his/her life. I believe that _____ thinks on things that are true, honest, just, pure, lovely, and of a good report. _____ is a person of purpose and great productivity, in Jesus' name, Amen.

Scriptures for Study

And all thy children shall be taught of the Lord; and great shall be the peace of thy children.

Isaiah 54:13

Be careful for nothing; but in every thing by prayer and supplication with thanksgiving let your requests be made known unto God.

Philippians 4:6

Being confident of this very thing, that he which hath begun a good work in you will perform it until the day of Jesus Christ.

Philippians 1:6

Then he said unto them, Go your way, eat the fat, and drink the sweet, and send portions unto them for whom nothing is prepared: for this day is holy unto our Lord: neither be ye sorry; for the joy of the Lord is your strength.

Nehemiah 8:10

Student With Special Needs

Father, thank You for perfecting everything that concerns me. Thank You for giving me a mouth and wisdom that the enemy cannot resist nor refute. I glory in You, knowing that You are the God who is more than enough in every situation. I lift up my student(s), with special needs to You. I believe they are more than conquerors and complete in You. Father, I have set all my students apart for the kingdom of God. I believe and confess that because they are of You, they have *already* overcome this disability. Greater is He who is in them than he who is in the world.

Father, I realize that labeling a child is man-made. It is a system designed by man to bring order to classrooms, to ensure all students get the best education possible without constant interruptions that may impede the educational process. It also serves to protect the students from failure and unfair punishment because of a disability. I thank You for the genuine efforts of these educational and medical professionals. They have the facts, but I believe Your Word holds the truth and the answer for this dilemma. I ask You to reveal Your plan to those who sit in authority in this area. I believe You are setting up believers to hear and do Your Word concerning this issue.

I speak deliverance to my student(s) _____who is/are overcoming genuine physical, mental, or emotional disabilities. I plead the blood of Jesus over _____ and command satan to desist in his attack against him/her.

Father, Your Word says that You would make the storm to calm. Therefore, I speak peace to my student(s) _____ who is/are temporarily experiencing hyperactivity, poor discipline, disrespect for authority, and poor grades. My student(s) _____ is/are taught of You, obedient to Your Word with great peace and undisturbed composure. Thank You for revealing to his/her parents and me the way of escape for he/she. My student(s) _____ commit his/her work unto You, his/her thoughts are established, and he/she experiences success in school and at home. I believe I have what I say and pray according to Your Word, in Jesus' name, Amen.

Scriptures for Study

The Lord will perfect that which concerneth me: thy mercy, O Lord, endureth for ever: forsake not the works of thine own hands.

Psalm 138:8

For I will give you a mouth and wisdom, which all your adversaries shall not be able to gainsay nor resist.

Luke 21:15

Nay, in all these things we are more than conquerors through him that loved us.

Romans 8:37

And ye are complete in him, which is the head of all principality and power:

Colossians 2:10

He maketh the storm a calm, so that the waves thereof are still.

Psalm 107:29

And all thy children shall be taught of the Lord; and great shall be the peace of thy children.

Isaiah 54:13

And this is the confidence that we have in him, that, if we ask any thing according to his will, he heareth us.

1 John 5:14

The Seven Success Practices for Teachers

1. **T**rust God.

   Trust in the Lord with all thine heart; and lean not unto thine own understanding.

   Proverbs 3:5

2. **E**xpect your students to succeed.

   According to my earnest expectation and my hope, that in nothing I shall be ashamed....

   Philippians 1:20

3. **A**void immorality and misconduct.

   That each one of you should know how to possess (control, manage) his own body in consecration (purity, separated from things profane) and honor.

   1 Thessalonians 4:4 AMP

4. **C**reate the atmosphere for all students to achieve.

   Love never fails.

   1 Corinthians 13:8 AMP

5. **H**one skills in classroom management.

   And all your [spiritual] children shall be disciples (*students*) [taught by the Lord and obedient to His will], and great shall be the peace and undisturbed composure of your children.

Isaiah 54:13 AMP

6. **E**ndeavor to include parents in the educational process.

For I know him, that he will command his children and his household after him, and they shall keep the way of the Lord.

Genesis 18:19

7. **R**eward students for their accomplishments.

The slothful...does not catch his game...but the diligent...gets precious possessions.

Proverbs 12:27 AMP

inspire for teachers

Wisdom
From Proverbs

Apples

Appealing Proverbs for Parents,
Leaders, Educators, and Students

Apples of Wisdom

God wants us to live successful lives. He did not create man to make him miserable. He created man to have fellowship with Him and dominion in the earth. God expects for us to rule over our situations and circumstances, not for them to rule us.

The path of education can, at times, be littered with unpleasant encounters. If you do not know God, His ways, or His Word, you may find yourself being overcome by what you should be overcoming.

Experiencing good success in this life can only be achieved through God's wisdom. Proverbs 4:7 tells us that wisdom is the principal thing. Wisdom teaches us God's ways and how to conduct ourselves in compliance with His will.

Wisdom is found in the Word of God. The book of Proverbs is known as the book of wisdom and was written "That people may know skillful and godly Wisdom and instruction, discern and comprehend the words of understanding and insight,

Receive instruction in wise dealing and the discipline of wise thoughtfulness, righteousness, justice, and integrity, That prudence may be given to the simple, and knowledge, discretion, and discernment to the youth—The wise also will hear and increase in learning, and the person of understanding will acquire skill and attain to sound counsel [so that he may be able to steer his course rightly.]" (Proverbs 1:2-5 AMP)

It is important for believers to give attention to the Word of God on a daily basis. Our natural man is fed daily and in like manner so should we feed our spirit man. Proverbs 4:20-22 talks about us giving attention to the Word and keeping it in the center of our hearts because it is life to us and medicine to our flesh.

A daily dose of the Word of God is the spiritual panacea for the ills of our schools and society. As a teacher or leader you need to engage in a daily regimen of reading and confessing the Word of God. Then you will experience peace (beyond your current imagination), length of days, and divine health.

The Reading Plan

The book of Proverbs has thirty-one chapters: a chapter for each day of the month. I recommend that you read chapter one on the first day of each month. On the second day of each month, read chapter two, and so on.

Confessions from each chapter have been provided. Confess the Word, audibly. As you make these confessions, they will reshape how you see yourself and thus you will become a mirror image of the Word of God. Remember Romans 10:9-10 says that confession is made unto (whatever you are confessing). For example, if you regularly confess that you have the peace of God, you will begin to operate in the peace of God.

WARNING: You are about to experience an Extreme Makeover by the power of God's Word. The following pages will change your life. Proceed with great expectation!

Proverbs Chapter 1

Student's Success

A wise man will hear, and will increase learning; and a man of understanding shall attain unto wise counsels.

Proverbs 1:5

Confess

My students hear and understand what I say, and so they increase in learning.

Wisdom

The fear of the Lord is the beginning of knowledge: but fools despise wisdom and instruction.

Proverbs 1:7

Confess

I fear the Lord which is the beginning of knowledge.

Protection

But whoso hearkeneth unto me shall dwell safely, and shall be quiet from fear of evil.

Proverbs 1:33

Confess

I hearken unto wisdom and I live safely without fear.

Proverbs Chapter 2

Success

My son, if thou wilt receive my words, and hide my commandments with thee; so that thou incline thine ear unto wisdom, and apply thine heart to understanding; yea, if thou criest after knowledge, and liftest up thy voice for understanding; if thou seekest her as silver, and searchest for her as for hid treasures; then shalt thou understand the fear of the Lord, and find the knowledge of God.

Proverbs 2:1-5

Confess

I receive the words of the Lord and store up His commands. I listen for His wisdom and apply it to my life. I seek God's counsel just like hidden treasure. I honor the Lord and find the knowledge of God.

Student's Success

When wisdom entereth into thine heart, and knowledge is pleasant unto thy soul....

Proverbs 2:10

Confess

Skillful and godly wisdom is in the heart of my students and knowledge is pleasant to them.

inspire for teachers

Wisdom

When wisdom entereth into thine heart, and knowledge is pleasant unto thy soul; discretion shall preserve thee, understanding shall keep thee: to deliver thee from the way of the evil man, from the man that speaketh froward things.

Proverbs 2:10-12

Confess

I have wisdom, knowledge, discretion, and understanding; therefore, I am delivered from what people say and do.

Proverbs Chapter 3

Success

My son, forget not my law; but let thine heart keep my commandments: for length of days, and long life, and peace, shall they add to thee.

Proverbs 3:1-2

Confess

I read, pray, meditate, and speak the Word of God and it adds length of days, long life, and peace unto me.

Favor

Let not mercy and truth forsake thee: bind them about thy neck; write them upon the table of thine heart: so shalt thou find favour and good understanding in the sight of God and man.

Proverbs 3:3-4

Confess

Because I bind myself to mercy and truth and keep them in my heart, I have favor and good understanding with God and with man.

Wisdom

Trust in the Lord with all thine heart; and lean not unto thine own understanding. In all thy ways acknowledge him, and he shall direct thy paths.

Proverbs 3:5-6

Confess

I trust in the Lord with all my heart, acknowledge Him in all my ways, and He directs my path.

Health

Be not wise in thine own eyes: fear the Lord, and depart from evil. It shall be health to thy navel, and marrow to thy bones.

Proverbs 3:7-8

Confess

I will not be wise in my own eyes. I honor the Lord and His commandments. I depart from evil and it brings health to my body.

Prosperous Life

Honour the Lord with thy substance, and with the first-fruits of all thine increase: so shall thy barns be filled with plenty, and thy presses shall burst out with new wine.

Proverbs 3:9-10

Confess

By giving of my increase to the Lord's work, I honor Him and He blesses me with abundance in all that I do.

Proverbs Chapter 4

Wisdom

Wisdom is the principal thing; therefore get wisdom: and with all thy getting get understanding. Exalt her, and she shall promote thee: she shall bring thee to honour, when thou dost embrace her.

Proverbs 4:7-8

Confess

I have embraced wisdom and it promotes and brings me to a position of honor.

Student's Success

I have taught thee in the way of wisdom; I have led thee in right paths.

Proverbs 4:11

Confess

I teach my students according to God's wisdom. I lead them in the right path.

Success

I have taught thee in the way of wisdom; I have led thee in right paths. When thou goest, thy steps shall not be straitened; and when thou runnest, thou shalt not stumble.

Proverbs 4:11-12

Confess

My path is clear and open; therefore, my steps shall not be hampered.

Health

My son, attend to my words; incline thine ear unto my sayings. Let them not depart from thine eyes; keep them in the midst of thine heart. For they are life unto those that find them, and health to all their flesh.

Proverbs 4:20-22

Confess

I read and meditate on the Word of the Lord. It is life to me and brings health to my body.

Wisdom

Keep thy heart with all diligence; for out of it are the issues of life.

Proverbs 4:23

inspire for teachers

Confess

I guard my heart from evil, for my heart determines the way of my life.

Proverbs Chapter 5

Student's Success

My son, attend unto my wisdom, and bow thine ear to my understanding: that thou mayest regard discretion, and that thy lips may keep knowledge.

Proverbs 5:1-2

Confess

My students exercise discretion. The wise answer to temptation is in their lips.

Student's Success

And thou mourn at the last, when thy flesh and thy body are consumed, and say, How have I hated instruction, and my heart despised reproof; and have not obeyed the voice of my teachers, nor inclined mine ear to them that instructed me!

Proverbs 5:11-13

Confess

My students love instruction and receive reproof. They obey my voice.

Proverbs Chapter 6

Wisdom

Thou art snared with the words of thy mouth, thou art taken with the words of thy mouth.

Proverbs 6:2

Confess

I will not be snared by my words because I always speak in agreement with the Word of God.

Prosperous Life

Go to the ant, thou sluggard; consider her ways, and be wise: which having no guide, overseer, or ruler, provideth her meat in the summer, and gathereth her food in the harvest.

Proverbs 6: 6-8

Confess

I am wise to make plans and provision for my future.

Proverbs Chapter 7

Success

My son, keep my words, and lay up my commandments with thee. Keep my commandments, and live; and my law as the apple of thine eye.

Proverbs 7:1-2

inspire for teachers

Confess

I keep God's commandments and live in success. The Word of God is the apple of my eye.

Proverbs Chapter 8

Success

I wisdom dwell with prudence, and find out knowledge of witty inventions.

Proverbs 8:12

Confess

The wisdom of God gives me good judgment and knowledge of creative and witty inventions.

Success

Counsel is mine, and sound wisdom: I am understanding; I have strength. By me kings reign, and princes decree justice. By me princes rule, and nobles, even all the judges of the earth.

Proverbs 8:14-16

Confess

I have the wisdom of God and I rule and reign wisely as an educational leader.

Student's Success

For whoso findeth me findeth life, and shall obtain favour of the Lord.

Proverbs 8:35

Confess

The favor of God is upon my life and the lives of my students.

Proverbs Chapter 9

Relationships

He that reproveth a scorner getteth to himself shame: and he that rebuketh a wicked man getteth himself a blot. Reprove not a scorner, lest he hate thee: rebuke a wise man, and he will love thee.

Proverbs 9:7-8

Confess

I will not argue with someone who mocks me, because it will do no good, but I can reason with a wise person; they will appreciate it.

Student's Success

Give instruction to a wise man, and he will be yet wiser: teach a just man, and he will increase in learning.

Proverbs 9:9

inspire for teachers

Confess

As I teach, my students increase in learning. They are wise beyond their years.

Health

The fear of the Lord is the beginning of wisdom: and the knowledge of the holy is understanding. For by me thy days shall be multiplied, and the years of thy life shall be increased.

Proverbs 9:10-11

Confess

I honor the Lord and receive wisdom; knowledge of Him gives me understanding. By Him my days are multiplied and years are added to my life.

Proverbs Chapter 10

Prosperous Life

He becometh poor that dealeth with a slack hand: but the hand of the diligent maketh rich.

Proverbs 10:4

Confess

I am diligent and it makes me rich.

Success

He is in the way of life that keepeth instruction: but he that refuseth reproof erreth.

Proverbs 10:17

Confess

I heed instruction and correction; therefore, I walk in the way of life and cause others to do the same.

Prosperous Life

The blessing of the Lord, it maketh rich, and he addeth no sorrow with it.

Proverbs 10:22

Confess

The blessing of the Lord makes me rich and adds no sorrow with it.

Proverbs Chapter 11

Wisdom

The integrity of the upright shall guide them: but the perverseness of transgressors shall destroy them.

Proverbs 11:3

Confess

I am a person of integrity and that integrity guides me.

Relationships

A talebearer revealeth secrets: but he that is of a faithful spirit concealeth the matter.

Proverbs 11:13

Confess

I refuse to gossip. I am of a faithful spirit and I keep the confidence of a friend.

Student's Success

The desire of the righteous is only good: but the expectation of the wicked is wrath.

Proverbs 11:23

Confess

I desire the best for my students.

Proverbs Chapter 12

Favor

A good man obtaineth favour of the Lord: but a man of wicked devices will he condemn.

Proverbs 12:2

Confess

Because I am truthful and try to do what's right instead of being manipulative, I receive favor from the Lord.

Success

A man shall be satisfied with good by the fruit of his mouth: and the recompence of a man's hands shall be rendered unto him.

Proverbs 12:14

Confess

The good work of my hands will come back to me.

Wisdom

Lying lips are abomination to the Lord: but they that deal truly are his delight.

Proverbs 12:22

Confess

The Lord delights in me because I speak the truth.

Proverbs Chapter 13

Wisdom

A man shall eat good by the fruit of his mouth: but the soul of the transgressors shall eat violence. He that keepeth his mouth keepeth his life: but he that openeth wide his lips shall have destruction.

Proverbs 13:2-3

Confess

By the words I speak, I enjoy many good things. I control what I say and it brings me a long life!

Success

Wealth gotten by vanity shall be diminished: but he that gathereth by labour shall increase.

Proverbs 13:11

Confess

I work hard and honestly and my wealth grows and becomes great.

Student's Success

The law of the wise is a fountain of life, to depart from the snares of death.

Proverbs 13:14

Confess

Teaching my students is a fountain of life that causes my students to avoid the traps of death.

Relationships

He that walketh with wise men shall be wise: but a companion of fools shall be destroyed.

Proverbs 13:20

Confess

I am wise because I spend time with others who are full of wisdom.

Proverbs Chapter 14

Wisdom

In the mouth of the foolish is a rod of pride: but the lips of the wise shall preserve them.

Proverbs 14:3

Confess

I refuse to speak in pride and my wise words preserve me.

Favor

Fools make a mock at sin: but among the righteous there is favour.

Proverbs 14:9

Confess

Fools may laugh about their sin, but because I am righteous I have favor.

Success

The simple believeth every word: but the prudent man looketh well to his going.

Proverbs 14:15

Confess

I am prudent in life and watch closely what I am doing.

inspire for teachers

Protection

In the fear of the Lord is strong confidence: and his children shall have a place of refuge.

Proverbs 14:26

Confess

I have strong confidence in the Lord and in Him I always have a place of refuge.

Proverbs Chapter 15

Relationships

A soft answer turneth away wrath: but grievous words stir up anger. The tongue of the wise useth knowledge aright: but the mouth of fools poureth out foolishness.

Proverbs 15:1-2

Confess

I use knowledge and wisdom to bless others by what I say.

Success

All the days of the afflicted are evil: but he that is of a merry heart hath a continual feast.

Proverbs 15:15

Confess

Even if trouble comes, I have a cheerful countenance and enjoy life.

Success

A man hath joy by the answer of his mouth: and a word spoken in due season, how good is it!

Proverbs 15:23

Confess

The answers I give bring me joy. I speak the right words at the right time.

Proverbs Chapter 16

Success

Commit thy works unto the Lord, and thy thoughts shall be established.

Proverbs 16:3

Confess

My work is committed to God, my thoughts are established, and my plans succeed.

Protection

When a man's ways please the Lord, he maketh even his enemies to be at peace with him.

Proverbs 16:7

Confess

My ways please the Lord. He makes even my enemies to be at peace with me.

Wisdom

Pride goeth before destruction, and an haughty spirit before a fall. Better it is to be of an humble spirit with the lowly, than to divide the spoil with the proud.

Proverbs 16:18-19

Confess

I refuse to be full of pride. I am of a humble spirit and I honor the Lord.

Student's Success

Pleasant words are as an honeycomb, sweet to the soul, and health to the bones.

Proverbs 16:24

Confess

I speak pleasant words that are as a honeycomb, sweet to the minds and healing to the bodies of my students.

Wisdom

He that is slow to anger is better than the mighty; and he that ruleth his spirit than he that taketh a city.

Proverbs 16:32

Confess

I have self-control, I am slow to anger and I rule my own spirit.

Proverbs Chapter 17

Relationships

He that covereth a transgression seeketh love; but he that repeateth a matter separateth very friends.

Proverbs 17:9

Confess

I choose not to gossip about a matter but instead to walk in love and forgive.

Wisdom

Whoso rewardeth evil for good, evil shall not depart from his house.

Proverbs 17:13

Confess

I reward the good work of my students.

Health

A merry heart doeth good like a medicine: but a broken spirit drieth the bones.

Proverbs 17:22

Confess

I have a joyful countenance and it keeps me healthy and strong.

inspire for teachers

Proverbs Chapter 18

Protection

The name of the Lord is a strong tower: the righteous runneth into it, and is safe.

Proverbs 18:10

Confess

God's name is a strong tower; I run into it and I am safe.

Favor

A man's gift maketh room for him, and bringeth him before great men.

Proverbs 18:16

Confess

My gift makes room for me and brings me before great men.

Relationships

He that is first in his own cause seemeth just; but his neighbour cometh and searcheth him.

Proverbs 18:17

Confess

I have wisdom and hear both sides of an argument before I decide who is right.

Wisdom

Death and life are in the power of the tongue: and they that love it shall eat the fruit thereof.

Proverbs 18:21

Confess

I speak life to my situations by speaking the Word of God concerning them.

Proverbs Chapter 19

Prosperous Life

He that getteth wisdom loveth his own soul: he that keepeth understanding shall find good.

Proverbs 19:8

Confess

I work to get wisdom because I love my own soul; I keep understanding and prosper.

Relationships

The discretion of a man deferreth his anger; and it is his glory to pass over a transgression.

Proverbs 19:11

Confess

I use self-control to keep my emotions in check and I earn respect by overlooking offenses.

Wisdom

Hear counsel, and receive instruction, that thou mayest be wise in thy latter end.

Proverbs 19:20

Confess

I accept correction. It makes me wise in times to come.

Success

There are many devices in a man's heart; nevertheless the counsel of the Lord, that shall stand.

Proverbs 19:21

Confess

I may have many ideas, but it is the Lord's purpose for me that will stand.

Proverbs Chapter 20

Relationships

It is an honour for a man to cease from strife: but every fool will be meddling.

Proverbs 20:3

Confess

I have honor and respect because I do not cause strife.

Student's Success

Even a child is known by his doings, whether his work be pure, and whether it be right.

Proverbs 20:11

Confess

My students are known by their doings, whether they are pure and whether they are right.

Success

Every purpose is established by counsel: and with good advice make war.

Proverbs 20:18

Confess

Before I make any big decisions, I seek out godly counsel; and so my purposes are established and successful.

Wisdom

Man's goings are of the Lord; how can a man then understand his own way?

Proverbs 20:24

Confess

My steps are ordered by the Lord and I refuse to worry about my future.

inspire for teachers

Proverbs Chapter 21

Prosperous Life

There is treasure to be desired and oil in the dwelling of the wise; but a foolish man spendeth it up.

Proverbs 21:20

Confess

When it comes to money, I use the wisdom of God and have great treasure.

Success

He that followeth after righteousness and mercy findeth life, righteousness, and honour.

Proverbs 21:21

Confess

I seek after and crave righteousness and mercy, which cause me to experience honor and the true meaning of living a successful life in the kingdom of God.

Success

There is no wisdom nor understanding nor counsel against the Lord.

Proverbs 21:30

Confess

The Lord is for me; and there is no human wisdom or understanding or counsel that can prevail against Him.

Proverbs Chapter 22

Protection

Thorns and snares are in the way of the froward: he that doth keep his soul shall be far from them.

Proverbs 22:5

Confess

I guard my soul and stay far from the snares of life.

Student's Success

Train up a child in the way he should go: and when he is old, he will not depart from it.

Proverbs 22:6

Confess

I train up my students in righteousness; and when they are older, they will not depart from it.

Student's Success

Foolishness is bound in the heart of a child; but the rod of correction shall drive it far from him.

Proverbs 22:15

Confess

A word of discipline will drive foolishness from the hearts of my students.

inspire for teachers

Success

Seest thou a man diligent in his business? he shall stand before kings; he shall not stand before mean men.

Proverbs 22:29

Confess

I am diligent and skillful in my business; therefore, I stand before people in high places and positions.

Proverbs Chapter 23

Success

For as he thinketh in his heart, so is he: Eat and drink, saith he to thee; but his heart is not with thee.

Proverbs 23:7

Confess

In my heart, I believe I am a successful teacher and/or leader; therefore, I am.

Success

Let not thine heart envy sinners: but be thou in the fear of the Lord all the day long. For surely there is an end; and thine expectation shall not be cut off.

Proverbs 23:17-18

Confess

I refuse to envy others. Instead, I honor the Lord at all times. I know He has a good plan for my life and my hope is secure.

Proverbs Chapter 24

Prosperous Life

Through wisdom is an house builded; and by understanding it is established: and by knowledge shall the chambers be filled with all precious and pleasant riches.

Proverbs 24:3-4

Confess

By wisdom I build my life. By good sense I establish my life. By knowledge I fill my life with precious and great riches.

Protection

If thou faint in the day of adversity, thy strength is small.

Proverbs 24:10

Confess

I will be strong in the day of trouble, for my strength is of the Lord.

Relationships

If thou forbear to deliver them that are drawn unto death, and those that are ready to be slain; if thou sayest,

Behold, we knew it not; doth not he that pondereth the heart consider it? and he that keepeth thy soul, doth not he know it? and shall not he render to every man according to his works?

Proverbs 24:11-12

Confess

If someone is headed for great trouble, I will not ignore it. I will try to stop them. The Lord knows my heart and will reward me for helping others.

Relationships

Rejoice not when thine enemy falleth, and let not thine heart be glad when he stumbleth: lest the Lord see it, and it displease him, and he turn away his wrath from him.

Proverbs 24:17-18

Confess

I refuse to rejoice when my enemies fall because it does not please the Lord.

Proverbs Chapter 25

Relationships

Debate thy cause with thy neighbour himself; and discover not a secret to another: lest he that heareth it put thee to shame, and thine infamy turn not away.

Proverbs 25:9-10

Confess

When talking with others, I refuse to betray the confidence of a friend. In that way, I keep my good reputation and my friend.

Success

A word fitly spoken is like apples of gold in pictures of silver.

Proverbs 25:11

Confess

I speak words in due season to people around me and it blesses everyone.

Student's Success

By long forbearing is a prince persuaded, and a soft tongue breaketh the bone.

Proverbs 25:15

Confess

In the midst of chaos, I am calm, and my soft speech breaks down the stubborn resistance of any student.

Protection

He that hath no rule over his own spirit is like a city that is broken down, and without walls.

Proverbs 25:28

Confess

I exercise self-control over my own desires and I am protected from trouble.

Proverbs Chapter 26

Relationships

Answer not a fool according to his folly, lest thou also be like unto him.

Proverbs 26:4

Confess

I avoid foolish conversations with foolish people, so that I do not become as a fool myself.

Relationships

Whoso diggeth a pit shall fall therein: and he that rolleth a stone, it will return upon him.

Proverbs 26:27

Confess

Any traps set for me will trap the people who set them.

Proverbs Chapter 27

Wisdom

Boast not thyself of to morrow; for thou knowest not what a day may bring forth. Let another man praise thee, and not thine own mouth; a stranger, and not thine own lips.

Proverbs 27:1-2

Confess

I refuse to boast about my future. I let others praise me instead of myself.

Protection

A prudent man foreseeth the evil, and hideth himself; but the simple pass on, and are punished.

Proverbs 27:12

Confess

I am discerning and smart. I foresee evil and take precautions to avoid it.

Relationships

Iron sharpeneth iron; so a man sharpeneth the countenance of his friend.

Proverbs 27:17

Confess

As iron sharpens iron, I sharpen the countenance of my friends.

Student's Success

Whoso keepeth the fig tree shall eat the fruit thereof: so he that waiteth on his master shall be honoured.

Proverbs 27:18

Confess

My students faithfully heed my instructions.

inspire for teachers

Success

Be thou diligent to know the state of thy flocks, and look well to thy herds. For riches are not for ever: and doth the crown endure to every generation?

Proverbs 27:23-24

Confess

I am diligent to know the state of my affairs. Inheritances and riches will not last forever, if no one is watching over them.

Proverbs Chapter 28

Success

The wicked flee when no man pursueth: but the righteous are bold as a lion.

Proverbs 28:1

Confess

I am the righteousness of God and as bold as a lion.

Wisdom

Evil men understand not judgment: but they that seek the Lord understand all things.

Proverbs 28:5

Confess

I seek the Lord's counsel and He helps me to understand all things.

Favor

He that covereth his sins shall not prosper: but whoso confesseth and forsaketh them shall have mercy.

Proverbs 28:13

Confess

I prosper and receive mercy because I confess and renounce my mistakes.

Protection

He that trusteth in his own heart is a fool: but whoso walketh wisely, he shall be delivered.

Proverbs 28:26

Confess

I walk in skillful and godly wisdom and I am delivered.

Proverbs Chapter 29

Student's Success

When the righteous are in authority, the people rejoice: but when the wicked beareth rule, the people mourn.

Proverbs 29:2

Confess

I represent righteous authority; therefore, my students are happy.

Success

Where there is no vision, the people perish: but he that keepeth the law, happy is he.

Proverbs 29:18

Confess

I have vision for the future and cast vision for my students. We will not perish.

Success

A man's pride shall bring him low: but honour shall uphold the humble in spirit.

Proverbs 29:23

Confess

I have a humble spirit; therefore, I obtain honor in every area of my life.

Proverbs Chapter 30

Protection

Every word of God is pure: he is a shield unto them that put their trust in him.

Proverbs 30:5

Confess

I put my trust in God and He is my shield.

Relationships

If thou hast done foolishly in lifting up thyself, or if thou
hast thought evil, lay thine hand upon thy mouth.

Proverbs 30:32

Confess

I refuse to exalt myself or plan evil, because it is shameful.

Proverbs Chapter 31

Wisdom

Give not thy strength unto women, nor thy ways to that
which destroyeth kings.

Proverbs 31:3

Confess

I do not give myself to habits or things that will destroy
my influence as an educator.

Wisdom

Open thy mouth for the dumb in the cause of all such as
are appointed to destruction. Open thy mouth, judge
righteously, and plead the cause of the poor and needy.

Proverbs 31:8-9

Confess

As a leader, God requires me to judge righteously and
help others.

Prayer of Salvation

God loves you—no matter who you are, no matter what your past. God loves you so much that He gave His one and only begotten Son for you. The Bible tells us that "whoever believes in him shall not perish but have eternal life" (John 3:16 NIV). Jesus laid down His life and rose again so that we could spend eternity with Him in heaven and experience His absolute best on earth. If you would like to receive Jesus into your life, say the following prayer out loud and mean it from your heart:

Heavenly Father, I come to You admitting that I am a sinner. Right now, I choose to turn away from sin, and I ask You to cleanse me of all unrighteousness. I believe that Your Son, Jesus, died on the cross to take away my sins. I also believe that He rose again from the dead so that I might be forgiven of my sins and made righteous through faith in Him. I call upon the name of Jesus Christ to be the Savior and Lord of my life. Jesus, I choose to follow You and ask that You fill me with the power of the Holy Spirit. I declare that right now I am a child of God. I am free from sin and full of the righteousness of God. I am saved in Jesus' name. Amen.

If you prayed this prayer to receive Jesus Christ as your Savior for the first time, please contact us on the web at **www.harrisonhouse.com** to receive a free book.

Or you may write to us at

Harrison House
P.O. Box 35035
Tulsa, Oklahoma 74153

About the Author

Dr. Josie Washington Carr has a love for God and a love for learning. She currently serves as an executive director of education. Throughout her twenty plus years in education, Dr. Carr has served as a teacher, principal, and special education coordinator.

Dr. Carr was formally educated at Texas Southern University in Houston, Texas. She holds an undergraduate degree in physical education, two masters degrees in special education and mid-management, and a doctorate in educational leadership.

Dr. Carr enjoys fulfilling her purpose in life through ministry and education, spending time with her family, and helping others to achieve their highest potential. She is the wife of Dr. Stanley Carr and the proud mother of Jarvis and Jakia Carr.

To contact Dr. Josie Carr,
please write to:
P.O. Box 672514
Houston, Texas 77267